Cheer on Your Team!

#52

Cheer on Your Team!

52 Tips to Increase Employee Retention, Engagement and Loyalty

JAN SPENCE

Cover design by Lewis Agrell
Illustrations by Jennifer Horton

For permissions contact:
info@janspence.com

CreateSpace
www.createspace.com

ISBN-13: 978-1724981325
ISBN-10: 1724981323

Printed in the United States of America

Contents

Dedication

This book is dedicated to my father, Dr. John E. Horton, Jr., and in memory of my mother, Mary Faye Wright Horton.

Thanks, Daddy, for giving me the gift of speaking and for being an example of learning names and caring about everyone we meet.

Thank you, Momma, for helping me to look for the Cindis of the world—those who are left out and need to see God's love, and for teaching me to live every day to the fullest.

Preface

As a little girl, I always dreamed of becoming a professional motivational speaker. The joy that comes from sharing knowledge and inspiring people to leave better than they arrived ignites the fire within me. Even as a young preacher's daughter at the age of six, I would deliver my "mini-sermons" from the small kneeling rail near the pulpit (the perfect height for a short Southern girl) while waiting for my dad to finish greeting the parishioners. I reveled in my "messages for Christmas" each December when I would lay on my tummy underneath our Christmas tree and tell stories and speak words of wisdom into the tape recorder to my imaginary audience. Since those early days, I've taken every opportunity to exercise my speaking skills. I finally made the decision after a long career in sales and running a small service business to "hang my shingle" as a speaker several years ago.

My first year, I spent the majority of my time networking locally, building relationships and jumping at every opportunity to get hired for training, keynote speaking or presenting breakout sessions at conferences. Not having a demo reel, seasoned content or an arsenal of client endorsements, I found that getting started was quite difficult. And depressing! The pressure I felt to have every tool that most veteran speakers have to promote themselves was overwhelming, to say the least. Waking up every morning knowing that I didn't have a video, a book, a blog, an online following, a strong social media presence, a training course and other products to sell after a presentation, a digital marketing campaign, bureau representation, a customer relationship manager database, a newsletter, a promotional brochure, a YouTube channel, a white paper, filmed television interviews, a media presence, and much, much more was exhausting and discouraging!

Near the end of that first year of very little paid work and a lot of prospecting, my extremely supportive husband, Mitch, suggested that maybe it was time to get a part-time job at the local grocery store while I continued to pursue my life's passion. Things just weren't happening as quickly as we had hoped. However, this suggestion was a big blow to my self-esteem and the belief that my dream would come true.

Finally, a month later, I booked my first paid keynote speech at a local organization's monthly meeting for $100. I had to beg them to pay me, explaining that the full-color glossy handouts were costing me $60 in printing costs alone!

A close friend drove from out of town to see me deliver this talk with plans to go to dinner afterwards. He's not one to freely give praise, yet he expressed how impressed he was, how engaged he was, how he didn't look at his phone once because I held his attention for an hour! He complimented my skills and the presentation. While I appreciated the affirmation, I told him through tears that I might need to get a part-time job because my progress was taking longer than expected. I just wasn't sure this career path was going to work—maybe it was time to switch gears.

But he dissuaded me from giving up on my dream. His words had power. They inspired me. He told me that he believed in me, that I had a gift that I had to share, and that I couldn't lose hope. He gave me ideas for ways to market myself more effectively and offered helpful advice while I was struggling. At the very moment I was ready to throw in the towel, he convinced me to persevere. His words of encouragement changed my path forever.

Now it was my turn to pay it forward. Countless others have been inspired and improved their lives as a result of the messages I've conveyed through my speaking and training business. For that reason, I wrote this book and share these 52 tips—to compel you to make a positive impact on those around you and to better equip you to do so.

Acknowledgements

Thanks to my husband, Mitch, for loving me for who I am—flaws and all—and for tirelessly supporting me living my dream, when I was able to cut myself a check and the many times I wasn't. I am grateful for your patience while taking my calls in the middle of your work day to help me work through some decision I needed to make and for listening to my indecisive banter as I navigated this business. You are the best "feedback form cutter" on the planet! Thank you for being true, giving me the life my heart has always longed for and for being my very best friend ever. I love you.

I want to thank my sisters, Jenny and Jamie, for their never-ending support and encouragement. Thank you for hours of "unpaid consulting" as my two favorite associates with Jan Spence & Associates, for last-minute wardrobe consults over FaceTime, for spending every Black Friday with me naked in a dressing room trying on outfits and for responding graciously to my "I'm training tomorrow, and I need a great illustration about X." Thanks to sister Jenny for all of your generous time and expertise given with handling all things graphic and marketing related in the business. It means so much that you illustrated this book! Thanks to sister Jamie for always keeping an eye out for cool props I can use for training and for that perfect blouse I can wear on stage.

Thanks to brother-in-law Jay for your expert editing skills, keeping me between the hash marks and for contributing your extensive football knowledge to the book. I appreciate your unique perspective and sharing openly to keep me relevant.

This would not be possible without Chief Rock Star Jaime—for keeping me sane. Thank you for your never-ending patience with my questions about things that I should know the answers to and for keeping me on task. Your support of our vision and mission to change the world through our organization and the countless hours you spent on this book mean the world to me.

There are so many others that I simply can't add all your names and reasons here. My gratitude extends to Billy Daubenmire, Linda Horton, Veronica Kosyakov, Lisa Yakobi, my master mind group, my business coach, my accountability partners, my extended family, my Bunco Babes, my Alpha Delta Pi sisters, the Jacksonville Dixie Blues coaches and teammates, my National Speakers Association family, and all of those who have encouraged me on my journey.

This book wouldn't be complete without expressing gratitude to Jesus Christ, my Lord and Savior. Thank you for my gifts, for helping to realize that my differences are okay—and even good—for encouraging me to keep persevering despite the challenge of building this business, and for keeping the rain away those days in May so I could write the bulk of this book. Thank you for giving me the courage to inspire others and do my part to change the world.

Introduction

I've never had a CEO call me to tell me that they have way too many employees engaged within their workforce, that productivity is at its peak, morale is too high, loyalty is over the top or turnover is way too low. After all, they're calling me for help!

Have you ever asked yourself these questions?

- "Why don't people just get along?"

- "Why doesn't everyone have the same enthusiasm for the organization that I do?"

- "Don't they know that if they just give a little more and exceed expectations, benefits will come?"

- "Can they not understand that there is a direct correlation between customer satisfaction and the success of the company?"

- "They should know that we care for them as a part of the business, so why don't they perform at a consistently high level?"

If these or other similar thoughts have crossed your mind, you're not alone. Increasing employee engagement, morale and loyalty is a challenge, yet critical to any institution's success. In an interview with Oscar-winning Pixar director, Brad Bird (*The Incredibles, Ratatouille*), he states, "In my experience, the thing that has the most significant impact on a movie's budget—but never shows up in a budget—is morale. If you have low morale, for every $1 you spend, you get about 25 cents of value. If you have high morale, for every $1 you spend, you get about $3 of value. Companies should pay much more attention to morale."[1]

Even though most executives are aware of this, they aren't quite sure what the best solution is. Typically, the human resources department is implored with the task to boost morale. While they work hard to rally the staff, this effort can be lost on those who cynically believe HR is "just doing their job," not understanding they truly care. In smaller organizations, improving morale falls on the shoulders of an overworked business owner who is just trying to keep the company afloat.

Now, imagine if your people see genuine effort from their peers and managers to encourage them? What if a colleague just randomly decides to offer an inside tip to a newcomer that makes their work life easier, with no expectation of a favor in return? What if a manager randomly applauds the team without the we-need-to-do-more speech at the end of the accolades? Or what if that struggling coworker receives praise from a peer for a small "win" just when they were ready to throw in the towel?

Most importantly, what if moments like these became habits—part of the company culture?

Words have profound power—they can elevate someone or tear them down. We should each choose our words wisely and realize that we, ourselves, can change the trajectory of another person's life. And our actions? They do indeed speak even louder. By being intentional about lifting others up, both when they are excelling and when they are struggling, we can influence the culture around us to transform into one of positivity, innovation and high performance. Do you have a story that might inspire others? I'd love to hear it. Email me at info@janspence.com, and you may be included in my next book or featured in a blog or presentation.

So how much difference will all this truly make? Think about it. We all crave human connection. Despite the fact that technology that has changed the methods through which we communicate, ultimately, we were created to connect with others on a more personal level. The beautiful interaction between human beings when hearts are inspired, spirits are lifted and minds are challenged to achieve more than they thought possible is, at its core, what drives innovation.

So how do we do this? Practice Cheer Leadership™! The story that follows will help you better understand this concept.

Cheer Leadership: The intentional encouragement and lifting up of others, both when they are doing well *and* when they are struggling, to increase morale, productivity and, therefore, profitability.

When was the last time you sent someone flowers? Was it that day on the calendar that prompts us each year? Was it a typical flower-sending occasion that reminded you to place that order? Or was it "just because"? Those random unexpected acts of kindness, gestures of appreciation and words of encouragement that are delivered when least expected are the ones that mean the most. That is the intention of Cheer Leadership—to use words and actions to lift someone up without necessarily having to have a reason to do so. Celebrate who people are, just as they are, and find reasons to shower them with appreciation and praise!

Haven't you been the recipient of these purely motivational moments? Who are those people in your life who have cheered you on? Contemplate how those words of belief in you, the gesture that came at just the right time, or the hand that lifted you up at a most critical moment had significant impact on your life's path. Whose statements or actions were pivotal in your journey? Who was instrumental in changing the course and direction of your life, career, decisions? Write down the names of your Cheer Leaders, those who have had a profoundly positive impact on you.

Name of Your Cheer Leader:
1.

2.

3.

Action or words spoken to you:
1.

2.

3.

Impact on your life:
1.

2.

3.

Age/year this occurred:
1.

2.

3.

Obviously, a key Cheer Leader in my life was that friend who took me to dinner after my first professional keynote presentation just when I was ready to give up on my career dream. His belief in my abilities, offer to help and words of encouragement changed the course of my life and others that I've influenced—forever.

You're reading this book for a reason. It is the rare leader who desires more stress! Studies reveal that 80 percent of workers feel stress on the job and nearly half say they need help in learning how to manage stress.[2] Deep down in your leadership soul, you want to make a difference and know that you can have greater impact on your team and organization. I believe that even if you selfishly want to create a more productive team so that you can profit career-wise, financially, or personally, you'll benefit by being a better Cheer Leader. I've not yet met a leader or employee who didn't desire being part of a team that has great morale, is cohesive and operates together smoothly. It's our human nature to be self-focused, so strive to be other-centered, and watch those you lead flourish even more. You'll feel good about it, and the recipients will remember your kind actions for a long time to come.

I hope the following story from my experience as a professional athlete will encourage you and further convince you that words and gestures *do* make a major difference—both in the workplace and, most importantly, in the lives of others. Ultimately people want to feel valued, be recognized and feel good about the work they are doing within the organization. By intentionally cheering on your team members, you will elevate the culture and their spirits, too.

So, here's my story.

It's Sunday, Aug. 19th, 2001, in Jacksonville, Florida, at 2:00 p.m., and it is hotter than a jalapeno's armpit!

I can see the field from my car in the parking lot and there are about 80 women there that day for the tryouts. They're every shape, color, size and flavor. I can see they're already warming up—stretching, sprinting and definitely sweating. I think, *There's no way I'm getting out of this air-conditioned car!*

But I go, and I notice something very strange. When I walk up, these 80 women are not talking to each other. *Eighty women are not talking to each other!* I can tell they are just focused on their own game. They're sizing each other up, strutting and glaring. That's because these 80 women are competing to be one of the first ever women's professional full-tackle football players for Jacksonville, Florida—the Jacksonville Dixie Blues!

I'm here today because I always wanted to play football as a little girl. I remember on Saturday afternoons, my mom would iron clothes while the Georgia Bulldogs played football on TV in the background. She'd say, "That looks like so much fun! I want to be on the field with the shoulder pads and the helmet and hit people!"

What she didn't realize is that her words were inspiring me. Her dream became my dream. But there was only one problem! There were no football teams for little girls. The closest I got to playing football was "2-4-6-8, who do we appreciate?" That's right! I was a cheerleader.

However, I carried that dream into my adult life. I can remember when my husband, Mitch, and I would be at the Jacksonville Jaguars games and I would echo the same words of my mother, "That looks like so much fun. I want to put on the shoulder pads and the helmet and hit people!" And he just seemed to ignore me ...

One Sunday afternoon in August, I'm sitting there on the den floor putting together a scrapbook. Of course, we have an NFL game on the TV in the background. Mitch is reading the Sunday newspaper when he asks me, "Jan, did you know that a women's football team is coming to Jacksonville, Florida?"

And I pop up and say, "You're kidding me!"

"No."

"Like with the shoulder pads and hitting?"

"Yeah."

"Like with the football helmet and the tackling?"

"Yeah."

"Just like the NFL?"

"Yeah."

"Wooohhhhh!"

I go into this dreamlike state, and I visualize myself practicing for the tryouts. I've got to pump iron to get strong and get fast at running the 40-yard dash. Oh, and I've got to learn all the rules. But what about game day? Game day! I can see myself running through the tunnel. There's the smoke and the lights; the crowd's cheering; I've got my shoulder pads and my helmet on! I've got that black stuff under my eyes.

As I come out of this fantasy I think, *I've got to do this.* I say, "Honey, when are the tryouts?"

"Soon. Real soon."

"Like how soon? Next year? Next month? Next week?"

"Today."

"What?"

"Today. In two hours."

And just like that, my dream vanishes.

Oh, well, I figure that's fine because I'm not really in shape to play football anyway!

But Mitch encourages me to go. I give him a hundred reasons why this is a very bad idea. I'm 5'2" tall. I'm 33 years old. I don't know how to throw a football. I don't know how to catch a football. I don't know all the rules. And, let's face it, the latest exercise I've been doing is Zumba and a little Jazzercise. But still my husband encourages me to go, and he challenges me. He says, "Honey, what's the worst thing that can happen if you go to the tryouts?" And I respond, "Well, I don't make the team." Then he asks, "What's the worst that happens if you don't go to the tryouts?" He knows the answer is that I will regret it for the rest of my life.

Then I remember these words from my mother, "Once an opportunity is gone, it's gone forever." So I go! I put on my gym clothes and grab my old softball cleats. As I leave, my husband sends me out the door with an entire Igloo cooler full of water and a case of Gatorade! How much does he think I can drink in two hours?

As I'm driving to the tryouts, I think, *You know what? I*

promised my hubby I would go to the tryouts, but I never said I'd get out of the car!

And after arriving: *I'm here, so why not? What do I have to lose? Besides my dignity!*

So I walk out onto the field. You should see these women. There is one—she's got to be 6'2". I'll call her Sasquatch. And then there's this compact little athlete. She's so fit, she's got to be a body builder. One woman is so fast, I think she's probably an Olympic sprinter. I'm thinking, *I sure could use a six-pack right now!* But I stay and the tryouts begin.

First, we do pushups. I hate pushups! I have not done a real pushup since field day in 7th grade! And then we do sit-ups. I mean the real thing! Not the fake little crunches we do in Jazzercise. Then we do the run and catch exercise. Of course, I miss the ball. Next, we do speed and agility drills, jumping drills, crawling drills, and, quite frankly, I pretty much perform them all at the same level—the bottom.

But then comes the 40-yard dash. I think, *I've failed at everything else. This is my chance! I've got to nail this one.* I'm getting pumped up! My adrenaline's running strong. I watch the other athletes go, and then it's my turn. The whistle blows, and I explode! My legs are going faster than they ever have before. In fact, I almost lose my balance, but I cross the finish line. I think, *I have done great! I crushed it! I feel awesome! I know my performance was spectacular!*

And then I hear these words from the sideline, "You are the weakest link! Is that the best you can do? Why do you even try?" Those words crush me. They humiliate me, and they defeat me. How can people be so cruel? I'm here pursuing my dream just like they are. Aren't women supposed to be supportive of other women? We finally have the opportunity of a lifetime and a chance to do something our mothers and grandmothers only dreamed of. We should be excited for one another, encouraging our sisters and sharing in the excitement of this momentous occasion. But that's not what's going on.

In that moment, in that pain, the experience brings back some childhood memories: I grew up in an athletic family—my dad was an all-round athlete, my mother a tennis pro who was inducted into her college Hall of Fame, my older sister an all-star in almost every sport and my younger sister excelled as a gymnast! And me? I didn't get that athletic ability. I was the cheerleader! I tried out for sports, but I hardly got to play. They let me play on the church league softball team, but always put me out in right field where no one ever hits the ball! I always felt left out, excluded.

Almost two decades later, here we go again. On that football field, in that moment, I'm that same kid.

Suddenly, a different kind of memory rushes into my mind: As a child I see my mother—the pastor's wife—leading a youth group in a damp basement in a small little church in South Georgia. She has all the kids in a circle and is explaining the rules. It's something like Hot Potato. They start to play.

Then my mother notices Cindi in the corner—you know, the girl that's a little awkward and never quite fits in. She's not playing. My mother stops the game. She walks over to Cindi. She puts her arms around her and leads her to the circle. Momma says, "Now, Cindi's here. We can all play," and the game begins.

At those football tryouts that day, I think of my mother's words and I make a choice: *I'm here now. And I choose to play—and not just play, I'm going to approach this like Momma would. But what do I have? What can I do to contribute to the team?* And then it hits me: T*hat Igloo cooler full of Gatorade and water!*

So I quickly retrieve the drinks and go up to another aspiring player on the sideline and introduce myself. I shake her hand, ask her name and offer her a Gatorade. Then I introduce myself to the next woman, then the one beside her and the next—I don't stop until I give out all of the Gatorade and water in my cooler.

Now, because I know their names, I start cheering them on and applauding. "Hey, nice hands, Jackie, nice hands!" "Good run, Chelley, good run!" Even when they mess up—*especially* when they mess up—I encourage them. "Sherine, you have got this, girl! You know you've got it," "Susan, just shake it off. You're just warming up, you can do it, girl!"

I acknowledge those who are doing well and encourage those who are struggling, in a place where no one had been saying such words.

Then I notice something beginning to happen. Something I didn't expect at these Jacksonville Dixie Blues tryouts. *Behavior is contagious.* Each of the women—one by one—begins to follow my lead. Soon they are all cheering for each other, applauding, high-fiving and laughing together. An hour ago, the only laughter I heard was at someone's expense. If someone fell, no one helped her up. Now you hear, "Come on back, Karen, come on back. You can take my spot. You can try again. You got this." Everyone is cheering everyone else on—and up—and we are performing and playing better as a result!

I wasn't their coach or their leader or even someone they knew. However, when I stepped onto the field that day, I used what I had—an Igloo cooler full of Gatorade and some words of encouragement—and the group was transformed.

That's not all. The coach noticed! In fact, he said, "Jan, you know what? We could use a person like you on our team." He recognized that what I had was just as valuable as Sasquatch's size, Brantley's reflexes or even Kim's speed. He realized that words of encouragement and acknowledgement were just as valuable as that athletic skill.

And that day, I became a pro football player!

Playing football for the Jacksonville Dixie Blues on special teams, I didn't score any touchdowns. I didn't make any earth-shattering plays. In fact, I wasn't even on the field that much. But I was on the sidelines cheering on my teammates, and we performed better because of it. In fact, we won the Atlantic Conference title and played in the Women's American Football League Championship Game our inaugural year.

When my mom encouraged young Cindi that day and when my husband's belief in me convinced me to go to the tryouts, I realized that with just a simple gesture (sharing a cold drink) or a kind word ("You can do it!") anyone could be included. If one woman—one rookie prospect—can change 80 competitors into teammates in one hour, what could we all do? What could you do? You don't need a genetic predisposition or to go to practice or even the gym! Just start today with what you have.

As a speaker, trainer, and business coach, I've dedicated my life to encouraging people through my words. Not just at work, but I also encourage people at the grocery store, at the gym, in the neighborhood and even at home. Be assured that I'm not talking about giving someone a blue ribbon just for showing up or condoning a lack of effort. I'm talking about real encouragement – looking someone in the eye, saying their name and letting them know that you believe in them and that they truly can and will perform better.

If you want to bring about a significant transformation in the performance, the culture and the morale of the people around you – your company, your customers, your organization, your school, your family or your community – the playbook is easy and the opportunities are endless. A word of encouragement is just a simple action and that behavior is contagious. If you cheer everyone on and up every day, everywhere, through the power of encouragement, your words, my words, our words will transform the world!

How to Make the Most Out of This Playbook

Expect your team to experience small incremental shifts over time, not to change miraculously overnight. By implementing these small, powerful tactics on a regular basis, you'll be amazed at the changes you see in a shorter amount of time than expected. Behavior is contagious! If I changed the dynamic of 80 women in one hour with applause, words of support and a simple, kind gesture like sharing a bottle of Gatorade, what impact could one person have on the whole company, just by starting with one of the following tips?

While many of these tips may be tailored to those in a leadership or management role, they can easily be translated into a peer-to-peer activity. For example, if the tip is to take the group to a ball game where the tickets might be purchased out of the company budget, you—as an associate—can easily organize collecting money and buying a set of group tickets in advance of the game. The point is to encourage and lift up your teammates. So get creative and think of ways to make this happen! Remember to email me at info@janspence.com with your unique Cheer Leadership stories so that I may include them in my next book!

Some of you may be thinking, *These are professional managers. Surely, they know how to encourage their team! Why would they need this book?* Well, if it was easy, everyone would be doing it! According to HR expert, Shawn Murphy—CEO and co-founder of WorqIQ—"The way organizations approach employee engagement is a problem. The wrong approach begins with an assumption—it starts with the top. While it's ideal to have leadership support from the top, the truth is that a company's CEO and other executives have only modest levels of influence on engagement. The true influencers are the managers at the mid-level.

"Research from Hay Group shows that an employees' immediate manager shapes 70 percent of their experience of work. That's big. A manager's leadership style has more meaning to employees than company benefits, peer relationship, project work, and even CXOs."[3]

This book is designed to help you get imaginative, mix things up, keep intentions fresh, keep the staff guessing and give you new ideas. What is easy to do is also easy not to do! For example, it's common knowledge what makes up a healthy diet—fruits, vegetables, lean protein, healthy fats—but obesity rates have tripled since 1975 according to the World Health Organization.[4] We know we should eat an apple a day, an easy thing to do, but we don't!

The Encouragement Scoreboard checklist in the back of the book is designed to keep you on track. We know that it is the consistent—even constant—small actions that have greatest impact over time. Although you may not use every idea in this book, I encourage you to use the concept of Cheer Leadership to get creative with what will work in your environment. I love new ideas, too, so please email me with your unique concepts so that they may be considered for the next book!

Visit janspence.com to get your special Cheer Leadership kit with tools to use in your workplace right away! Watch for upcoming Cheer Leadership books geared toward specific groups such as salespeople, non-profits, associations, neighborhoods, families, faith-based organizations and more!

I would love the opportunity to personally inspire your team—just invite me in for a keynote, workshop or ongoing team huddle. Find out more about Jan Spence & Associates' speaking, training and consulting services by visiting janspence.com, emailing info@janspence.com or calling 904-821-9309.

1. Food Fair Catch

An apple a day keeps the doctor away. Wouldn't the team be surprised (and extremely excited!) if you were to walk in with a homemade apple pie that was baked using your grandmother's world-famous recipe?

If you want to win favor with people, the fastest way is through their stomachs! Whether you're making your own special dish from scratch or baking Pillsbury Slice 'n Bake chocolate chip cookies, they're sure to warm up any team. This Cheer Leadership tip goes straight from the stomach to the heart! We love to know how people are putting these tips into action, so send us photos of your team and the recipe, and you may be included in our next book! Email us at info@janspence.com to share.

Rookie Advice: Picking up donuts from the local bakery is always welcome; however, there is something unique and meaningful when the staff knows that you took the time in your personal life to buy the ingredients and labor in the kitchen with them in mind.

Pro Tip: While the kitchen is messy, why not make several batches of your Uncle Phil's famous lumpia or your brother Billy D's Bundt cake ahead of time and freeze them? Then they're easy to grab and go, and the office will never know the difference.

2. "I Spy" Immaculate Reception

I spy with my little eye! Be intentional about taking the "I Spy" approach with your people. It's easy to get caught up in the day-to-day grind. We all have more work, responsibilities, requests for our time, and demands on our performance than ever before. Technology has made our lives easier in many ways, but it's also brought us more distraction and disruption.

It's easy to stay in the coach's corner and not go out in the field unless you're urgently needed to put out a fire. This one takes intentionality to catch your people doing things *right*—going above and beyond! When you "spy" on them and see a behavior, attitude, or action that excels and is out of the norm, be sure to mention it in person. This is particularly meaningful when you have a team member that is struggling. Acknowledging and calling out what they are doing well has incredible impact on their morale—and the way they view you as a leader.

When Glassdoor and Harris Interactive surveyed more than 2,000 U.S. adults in 2013, they found that four out of five employees were motivated to work harder when their boss showed them appreciation.[5]

Look them in the eye, use their name, and sincerely thank them by identifying the specific behavior, action, or attitude they exhibited that deserves praise. Tell them how much you appreciate the effort and what it means to you, the customer, the team, the company, etc. Noticing and acknowledging improved behavior will have that underperforming staffer craving those accolades so that they repeat what warranted it to begin with. It will also increase their respect for—and personal loyalty to—you.

The Immaculate Reception: one of the most famous plays in NFL history, which occurred on December 23, 1972 during a playoff game between the Pittsburgh Steelers and the Oakland Raiders. With the Steelers behind and less than 30 seconds left in the game, Pittsburgh quarterback Terry Bradshaw attempted a pass to John Fuqua. The ball was knocked into the air, and Steelers running back Franco Harris appeared to catch it and ran the ball in for the game-winning touchdown. There is controversy to this day about how the ball was deflected and whether or not Harris caught it before it touched the ground.[6]

3. Gridiron Greeting Card

The age-old company is called Hallmark for a reason. Be that person in the office who leaves a card on someone's desk "just because." Remembering birthdays and special events is great, but a card telling them how much you appreciate them for the job they do means even more. It is especially welcomed when someone is overwhelmed at work, lost that big account or is going through a tough time personally. Cheer Leadership is being intentional when your compadre is struggling. That's when they need to be remembered and uplifted the most.

> **Pro Tip:** Buy a bunch of cards in advance. Dollar stores have some great, funny cards and plenty of generic ones for all occasions. Get these and more in your Cheer Leadership kit at janspence.com.

Gridiron: another name for football field, originating from the late 19th century and early 20th century. The term comes from the fact that original football fields were marked by a checkerboard pattern (versus the yard lines and hash marks we are accustomed to seeing today), which resembled a metal grid used to cook over fire (i.e. a gridiron).

4. Plant Playmaker

Give a plant to that person who is having a tough time adjusting to the company or just doesn't get much praise or attention. Research shows that plants take toxins out of the air, can reduce workplace illness and can help us be more creative![7] You'll be surprised how focusing on the minimal care that it takes to maintain a plant on an ongoing basis gives that person a sense of belonging and purpose.

Peace lilies, parlor palms, philodendrons and snake plants are some of the best low-maintenance and shade-friendly varieties and are perfect for office settings. Greenery makes an office a more pleasant environment, therefore lowering blood pressure and decreasing stress according to one study.[8] While it is a small thing, you'll be thought of every time Marcos waters that perennial. Often, he'll go the extra mile for you especially because you took the time to show you cared.

FUN FACT! In the November 2, 1898 football game between Princeton and the University of Minnesota, six male cheerleaders entertained the crowd for the first time. They were led by Minnesota student Johnny Campbell, and this date is considered the birth of cheerleading. [9]

5. Quote Quick Snap

One of my favorite things to do at a party or even at a casual gathering of family and friends is to start a written list of "memorable statements." Some of my all-time favorites are "This wine smells like my grandfather's dirty socks," "Where did you get your San Francisco t-shirt?" and, the reigning leader, "Never feed a horse Vienna Sausages." By paying attention and capturing these sound bites of life, we are immortalizing those joyous moments together.

This fun, easy tactic can be replicated at work! Start making that list on your phone or have the entire staff contribute on the breakroom whiteboard. Select the "quote of the day," "phrase of the week," or "sound bite of the month" where you highlight the most memorable statement, question, or comment. This is a way to bring some fun and levity to the office environment by making note of the everyday bloopers, wisdom, and yes, even customers' most outrageous comments that come from the sidelines. Remember to avoid using quotes that will make an employee feel embarrassed.

FUN FACT! Don Shula holds the record for the most career game wins in National Football League history. Bill Belichick (currently in third place for the record) would need seven consecutive 10-win seasons to pass Don Shula on the list for most coaching victories! [10]

Be sure to keep an ongoing list, as this makes for great fodder for your annual speech at the company holiday party! People always feel special when you remember and recall what they said that was momentous. Many of these quips will soon become company mantras! Inside jokes build unity and foster inclusiveness and bonding within a team. Remember to email us at info@janspence.com with some of your best comments, and they may be included in our next book!

6. Just Smile

There are many ways to be intentional with this tip. One way is when you're delivering challenging news to the team, deliberately smile to soften the blow. Sadly, so many people are not intentional about using this simple facial gesture to communicate joy and happiness. Consider Albert Mehrabian's widely respected communication formula: 55 percent of communication is body language, 38 percent is tone of voice, and only seven percent is the actual words people use.

However, as Mehrabian further explains in his book *Nonverbal Communication:* "When there are inconsistencies between attitudes communicated verbally and posturally, the postural component should dominate in determining the total attitude that is inferred."[11] We conclude from his research that the facial expression of a smile communicates more than the words being said.

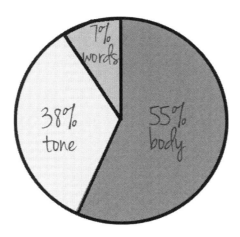

One way to be intentional with this tip is when delivering challenging news to the team, deliberately smile and that will soften the blow. You will subliminally cheer on your team by subconsciously communicating that everything is going to be fine. Your smile transfers confidence as the quarterback of the team who has the best interest of the players at heart. As you exude positivity, the team will rally about the possibilities going into the next quarter! While this impact may be hard to detect, if you are paying attention, you'll notice a quiet calm as the team enters the game with a solid confidence with you as their leader.

Rookie Advice: It's best to smile consistently; however, there are some exceptions. Be sensible about this. You wouldn't deliver "You're all fired!" with a grin on your face. Well, maybe you would, but that's an entirely different topic!

7. The Lateral

"Spend a day in the life of ..." Well, okay, maybe an hour with Jane would suffice, depending upon her job role. As Mary T. Lathrap put it in her 1865 poem *Judge Softly*, "Before you judge a man, walk a mile in their moccasins." It is so easy to forget your humble beginnings or even appreciate what a "day in the life" is for those who serve in various roles. If it's been a while since you worked in her department or if you have never walked in her shoes, you'll gain great insight by doing so.

Schedule time on your calendar to "walk alongside" these valuable jobholders so that you can appreciate what their day-to-day work life is really like. While this may make Jane a bit self-conscious, she'll ultimately appreciate the intentionality you put into "understanding her world." Perhaps invite her to select the time so you can see her at her busiest or, in her perspective, the best part of her day. You'll be amazed at what you'll learn about how your employees interact, what processes are in need of improvement, what inefficiencies still exist even though you have resources, who on the team might need a "timeout" to avoid burnout, where shrinkage could be avoided, where time could be maximized, and who has potential and skill sets you were unaware of because they've been hiding them under a bushel basket in their cubicle!

> **Rookie Advice:** With this form of Cheer Leadership, be mindful that you are not there to correct or critique Jane! You are there to *observe*. Seek first to understand! Let her know that you aren't there checking up on her, but rather to better understand what a "day in the life of Jane" looks like. As a leader, you want to stay in touch

with changing job duties and be there to support them when welcomed change is warranted and needed. This "ride along" should be seen as supportive and not critical to avoid any defensiveness in the future.

8. The Heisman Trophy

Pass around a trophy as a weekly award to the crew member that excels. This can be a plastic trophy from the dollar store, a stuffed animal mascot, or any other icon that can be proudly displayed (even if it looks a little silly).

Rookie Advice: In many organizations a matrix is *already* in place to reward meeting expected benchmarks of the job i.e. net promoter scores, customer satisfaction, online or phone surveys about customer service, sales goals, packages shipped on time, minimized errors, etc. These are already part of the expectation of performing the job. Praise for meeting these goals should still be part of your Cheer Leadership game plan, and this tip is for rewarding behavior when someone goes all out and leaves it all on the field.

Pro Tip: Have personnel nominate the winner for the week in a typical secure suggestion box. All you have to do before the appointed weekly time is:

1. Sort through the suggested nominees (and reasons for being nominated).
2. Award the most timely, appropriate candidate.
3. Save the others for upcoming weeks if needed!

Use a spreadsheet or "Hall of Fame" wall to keep track of the weekly winners. This visible competition is sure to drive whatever character traits or squad behavior you are choosing as the criteria for winning the nomination. This could be teamwork, taking extremely good care of a challenging customer, running interference for an absent co-worker, or going above and beyond the call of duty. Get these tools and more in your Cheer Leadership kit at janspence.com.

9. Timeout

Take a random break from work and energize your team with a timeout (and this isn't the one you use to put your three-year-old in a corner as punishment!). Recent studies show that those who give in to some kind of diversion or distraction once an hour perform better than those who just keep at it without a break. After a while, our brains numb out a bit to the constant stimulation, and we become unable to continuously treat the task as important. Taking a break allows us to come back to the job at hand with renewed energy and sense of purpose. [12]

Ideas for this Cheer Leadership tip: Walk around the block, throw a frisbee in the park, play a game of solitaire or a video game, or anything else that allows your brain to "check out" for a few minutes. Get creative and have fun! Remember to email us at info@janspence.com with photos of the ingenious ways your team decides to do this so we can share.

FUN FACT! It's reported that University of Minnesota student Johnny Campbell's first cheer was, "Rah, Rah, Rah! Ski-u-mah, Hoo-Rah! Hoo-Rah! Varsity! Varsity! Varsity, Minn-e-So-Tah!" This apparently led to the popular "sis boom bah" cheer. Campbell is widely considered the original cheerleader.[13]

10. The Huddle

Make time in staff or departmental meetings for personal sharing. Remember that employees are people with emotions, challenges, families, and lives outside of work. Find out more about what makes them tick so you can establish a deeper connection with those you lead and serve alongside.

Many studies have been done on the value of having "workplace friends" where relationships go beyond the typical nine to five grind.[14] According to Reuben Yonatan's research, benefits include:

- Increased emotional well-being
- Improved job satisfaction
- Decreased stress
- More effective teams
- Increased productivity
- A healthier heart!

Rookie Advice: While learning about another's personal life deepens connections, be careful that this time of sharing does not turn into one employee's personal therapy session. Depending upon the culture of the company, your troop should be encouraged to be vulnerable, open and frank. However, there should still be a level of professional decorum regarding what is acceptable to share, how, and when. In addition to briefly explaining parameters, leading by example in this exercise will be key.

11. Name The Formation

One of the simplest, easy, no-cost actions of Cheer Leadership is also one that many people forget or simply haven't made into a habit.

This overlooked technique is one that has powerful subconscious potential to connect and bond people together. Instead of the usual "Good morning" to the corporate receptionist, try "Good morning, Akeem" for a more relational touch. Using an individual's name along with eye contact increases the level of personalization and specificity so that it's a meaningful interaction. You'll be the first to get notified of important messages by acknowledging this new fan.

In Dale Carnegie's timeless book *How to Win Friends and Influence People* he wrote, "If you want to win friends, make it a point to remember them. If you remember my name, you pay me a subtle compliment; you indicate that I have made an impression on you. Remember my name and you add to my feeling of importance." We feel more valued and respected when someone remembers our name. We feel more engaged in a conversation when someone uses our name. Carnegie further adds, "A person's name is to him or her the sweetest and most important sound in any language."[15]

Formation: the strategic positioning of players on the field by the offense, defense or special teams right before each play begins.

12. Sticky Note Sneak Play

This tip is so easy, yet so meaningful to the recipient. Hide a sticky note with a word of encouragement somewhere on your teammate's desk—in a drawer, filing cabinet, under their printer lid, under their locker door or even on the computer monitor. You'll be the highlight of their day!

This is especially appreciated when someone is struggling or going through a tough time at work or at home. You don't even need to sign your name to express this type of Cheer Leadership.

Don't know what to say? Something as simple as "You're doing a great job!" "We appreciate you!" or an inspiring quote or profound proverb will be sure to create a loyal fan (should you choose to sign it) with this little surprise! We'd love for you to email us (info@janspence.com) your video of you hiding your "sneak plays" around the office. Better yet, catch someone on film finding that treasure!

> **Sneak Play:** also known as a trick play, these are rarely used football plays because they are risky and typically don't follow the usual strategy by a team. They almost always involve elements of surprise and deception.

Of course, these were my favorite plays as a member of special teams!

13. Send A Meal Sweep

Got a co-worker out on injured reserve for a few days? We all love the comfort of chicken noodle soup when we're under the weather. No need to mess up the kitchen to be intentional about this Cheer Leadership tip. It's easy to send a hot bowl right to the worker's doorstep. Just go online and schedule the home delivery within minutes. Panera Bread Company restaurant has great chicken noodle soup and provides delivery within certain areas for a nominal $3 fee.

There are many other general delivery services available such as:

· Doorstep Delivery (DoorstepDelivery.com)
· GrubHub (GrubHub.com)
· Bite Squad (BiteSquad.com)
· DoorDash (DoorDash.com)
· UberEats (UberEats.com)

If you're able to let Jacinda know food is on its way, even better! If not, imagine her surprise that you took the time to care when she was out of the office.

> **Sweep:** a running play in football where the running back gets the ball from the quarterback and starts running parallel to the line of scrimmage. His linemen head the same direction and get in front of him to block defenders before he turns toward the end zone.

Here are three great options to make scheduling meals easier than ever!

- MealTrain.com
- TakeThemaMeal.com
- SignUpGenius.com

Pro Tip: For other instances where teammates may be out of the office (surgery, death in the family, maternity leave, etc.), sending a meal or platter for the whole family is greatly appreciated. For longer term absences, use online meal schedulers when the workforce in the office is willing to chip in and make and take meals to help. Many will love that no meal prep is required because most websites allow for a donation or ordering of a particular meal online!

14. Candy Bar Quarterback Draw

Uncover what your cohort's favorite candy bar is and show up first thing in the morning with this little pick-me-up, especially after a tough game. The personal knowledge of knowing their favorite brings real connection and will make you stand out from the crowd. After all, Dr. Drew Ramsay, a physician who specializes in brain health wrote: "Sugar is vital for your brain health—which is the biggest guzzler of the sweet stuff in your body, FYI."[16]

Quarterback Draw Play: an offensive play that appears to the opponent as if it will be a pass, but the quarterback tucks the ball and runs through a gap in the line after dropping back as if to pass.

15. Puppy Pro Bowl

Who could possibly have a bad day when staring into the eyes of a fuzzy, cuddly puppy? Find the appropriate time to bring your furry friend to work for a time and observe as the weight of the world melts away before your very eyes. If you or your fellow troop-members don't have one, it's easy enough to find a local pet therapy organization where you can schedule a visit from our four-legged friends. Check out PetPartners.org to connect with an organization near you!

> **Pro Tip:** If you are a larger organization where there might be multiple personnel who would adopt a pet, contact your local pet shelter to schedule an adoption day. In many cases, they will bring the animals in need of adoption to your location. Once your staff falls in love, they will provide much-needed homes for these precious creatures!

FUN FACT! Cheerleading is over 100 years old. In the beginning, all cheerleaders were men.[17]

16. Supervisor Legal Substitution

As a colleague, your team wants to have confidence in your capabilities and your leadership ability to guide the team, but they don't want to feel as if they are in competition with their coach! No one likes a power monger or a "show boat," that one on the team that thinks that they are better than everyone else, AKA Mr. Smarty-pants or Ms. Prisspot. Avoid being that person! It is one thing to say, "Would it be okay with you, Jade, if I offered a different approach to this task? I've seen it work really well." versus "Let me show you how I did it back in the day! I am amazing! I am magnificent! I am a star!" Confidence and capability should not be confused with arrogance and a braggadocios attitude.

Be purposeful in sharing the leadership role. Find opportunities on a frequent basis where members of your team can step outside of their normal job and take on a different, challenging role or task that you typically handle as the coach. This increases their investment in the organization as they experience the responsibility that you have as the manager and brings their own perspective to this temporary role. This will also help identify potential leaders and rising stars, soon to be MVPs, who can grow into team captains within the company.

Research shows that personnel who are considered for a more senior role are more aligned with the company's vision and will strive for company growth over the long term. Hiring from within is almost always more cost-effective than bringing in outside talent and the ramp up time is typically shorter as well.[18]

Pro Tip: For example, you may be in charge of writing a report on the department's latest accomplishments for the company newsletter or asked for input for the safety improvement task force. The trust that you instill in them by having them "sub" for you and tackle an assignment that is ordinarily relegated to a supervisory role will gain yardage in the mind of the selected player.

Legal Substitution: While almost every player substitution that you see in football is "legal," an offense is penalized for *illegal* substitution if it has twelve players in its huddle at the same time. A defense is penalized for it if it has twelve players on the field when the ball is snapped—even if one is in the process of running off the field.

17. Eligible Receivers on the Elevator

We all get numb to the everyday surroundings of our environment. Posting a handwritten poster or banner rooting for your team in the elevator (or in the break room, by the time clock, on the front entry door—wherever everyone will pass by) will catch their attention.

You don't have to run around to everyone's office with a fan's foam finger, but your words of praise will be noticed when they are sincere. Let's face it, not everyone pours through the company newsletter to read accolades on who did what last month. This will get their attention and comes from the heart. So grab your paper and markers and congratulate your team! Remember to send us a photo of your creative banner to info@janspence.com so we can share your ideas.

Rookie Advice: Be sincere. When you are able to identify the specific activities and accomplishments of the troop, it will be more meaningful. As with rewarding trophies, it is best when this accolade identifies a group challenge that has been overcome versus reaching expected sales goals.

18. Cultural Crowd Pleaser

With so many generations, cultures and backgrounds in the shop these days, there is much to celebrate with our diversity and uniqueness. Everyone loves to share fond representations of their background, heritage, culture or hometown. Whether it's wearing your old jersey from that beloved, award-winning hometown team, making the famed traditional corned beef and cabbage from the old country or sharing that green hatch chile salsa that your homeland is known for, it brings joy to all to share a little slice of who they are.

Plan a good ol' potluck meal where each member of your team brings a dish to share which represents their heritage. The variety will be amazing! Stories about recipes and memories surrounding these foods will be shared with joy and fondness. This time of bonding over cuisine and getting to know each other in a different way will long be remembered as one of the highlights of the game!

FUN FACT! Women joined cheerleading squads in 1923. During World War II when so many young men were away, the shift to mostly female cheer squads began. [19]

19. Pom-Pom Props

Acknowledging and recognizing milestones can go a long way in making someone's day. Whether it's a birthday, a work anniversary, a promotion or some other professional accomplishment, hearing the words "Happy Birthday" or "Congrats" are sure to spread a spirit of positivity in your office. Get creative and find unusual reasons to celebrate life with your co-workers such as "Congrats on your new puppy!" or "You survived your first tax season!" In my book, just making it to Friday is reason enough to celebrate!

> **Pro Tip:** Stock up on cards and keep them at work so you're ready to cheer someone on when the occasion arises. Even blank ones with cool or beautiful images on the front will do for this play. As you begin to be intentional about looking for opportunities to practice Cheer Leadership, you'll notice more and more circumstances to reward, honor and recognize your peers. Don't delay when that idea to cheer someone on pops in your head. Just as in the game of football, you should take action immediately. You'll be rewarded for your speed! Get these tools and more in your Cheer Leadership kit at janspence.com.

20. Poem Pooch Kick

I'm not sure that I've met many people who actually look forward to the regular, often boring, staff planning meetings. Break things up with the occasional mindbender. Pick a current office topic, pair up people who don't typically work closely together and have them create a limerick on the subject. Here's how:

A limerick is a humorous poem consisting of five lines. The first, second and fifth lines must have seven to ten syllables and must rhyme. The third and fourth lines only have to have five to seven syllables and will rhyme with each other.

Examples are actually some well-known rhymes:

"Hickory, dickory, dock,
The mouse ran up the clock.
The clock struck one,
And down he run,
Hickory, dickory, dock."

"When writing a limerick five
Is the number of lines to contrive,
To write more or less
The rule would transgress
And our art of perfection deprive."

Wonderful, healing laughter will ensue at hearing the creativity (or lack thereof!) from fellow staffers.

There is scientific proof that laughter really is good medicine! A Vanderbilt University study estimated that just 10-15 minutes of laughter a day can burn up to 40 calories. Meanwhile, a University of Maryland study found that a sense of humor can protect against heart disease. [20] We love to laugh, too, so be sure to email us at info@janspence.com with your team's laughable limerick!

Pooch Kick: a short, low, line kick in which the ball bounces around before it is picked up by a player from the receiving team; it can also be known as a squib kick.

21. Concession Stand Cheat

Popcorn! There's just something about popcorn that permeates any environment and immediately brings happy thoughts to mind. Take a freshly-popped break and personnel will come running down the field. For those that don't come with outstretched arms, drop off a little bowl at each person's desk. It's irresistible and will lift everyone's spirits amidst a stressful day. Just because you care, show them some freshly-popped love!

FUN FACT! About 98 percent of all female cheerleaders were former gymnasts, compared to just 20 percent of all male cheerleaders. [21]

22. Rookie Orientation

It's never easy being the "newbie" at work. Imagine their first impression when they show up at the office to a "Welcome, Jada!" banner hanging on the entry wall or in their cubicle! Take them to lunch or ask them to join you for a cup of coffee and introduce them to other employees.

One of my clients sends a "Getting to Know You" form to new employees before their start date. Because they work remotely, they travel to the home office for their orientation. Imagine the surprise when Spencer walks into his hotel room to find his favorite beverage on ice, his favorite snacks and candy and a gift certificate to his favorite restaurant! Already, the score begins to soar in the company's favor! In addition, he is getting a glimpse into the caring culture and feeling part of the team.

Another company has existing personnel show up early on the day a new hire starts and instructs the newbie to arrive a half hour later. Most new employees will arrive early anyway. As the rookie walks in the door, they are greeted with a red carpet, a welcome banner and cheers and applause from their new fellow teammates. A framed photo of the employee with their family or their pet awaits them in their new office. (It's easy to request this by email at the same time you send new employee paperwork in advance of their start date. Let them know it's for a special surprise on their first day.) Who wouldn't be a raving fan after the first day with this kind of kickoff? Remember to email us at info@janspence.com with your original ideas and photos so you may be included in our next book!

23. Cuban Coffee Combine

This tip comes from my Cuban friends here in Florida. It is customary in Cuba for any coworker to make a pot of hot espresso, pour it in little tiny shot-sized cups, put a dozen or so on a tray and walk around the office offering the afternoon "pick me up." I love this tradition!

Also known as "Cuban shot" or "Cuban pull," if you don't quite have those tools on hand for this specific caffeine-laden expression of appreciation, there are other creative options. What about emptying the vending machine for a selection of popular soft drinks or stock up on high-test carbonation from the store, throw them in your rolling Igloo cooler and stroll the building offering refreshment just when you feel everyone needs an extra boost?

> **Pro Tip:** Plan in advance and create a Gatorade break to give everyone just the energy hydration boost they need. Right in the middle of inventory, Black Friday shipping, or the end-of-the-month reporting push, that thirst quencher will be appreciated! You know the crunch times for your office when tension is high and the pressure is on, so prepare ahead.

A little energy boost helps to get the team through the 4th quarter. An alternative to offering drinks is to offer energy foods like bananas, almonds and protein bars to keep those blood sugar levels even. Studies show that protein can improve our concentration, increase energy, boost absorption of important nutrients, and bolster clarity and creativity. [22]

24. Training Camp

Get moving! In many work environments, physical movement isn't a regular part of the daily routine. Research clearly shows that sitting for long periods of time isn't healthy for us. In fact, standing up and walking around for just five minutes every hour during the workday could lift your mood, combat lethargy without reducing focus and attention, and even dull hunger pangs. [23]

I recommend using this tip repeatedly, at least once a month, as a team. Find a time to take an impromptu exercise and movement break. Call everyone into the conference room, pop in that Jillian Michaels DVD, get moving and start laughing! Invite a chair yoga specialist to come in and lead a session or find videos online that will help your team relax, rejuvenate and renew the body and mind.

> **Pro Tip:** You've probably heard of the yoga pose "downward facing dog," but did you know of the "desk upward dog"?

Here are several resources:

verywellfit.com/yoga-stretches-at-your-desk-3567200
entrepreneur.com/article/279988
more.com/lifestyle/exercise-health/10-yoga-stretches-do-your-desk
mayoclinic.org/healthy-lifestyle/adult-health/multimedia/stretching/sls-20076525

Almost every office has the resident fitness expert (your team trainer)—you know who they are! Have them lead the team in a series of stretches to loosen up tense muscles, get oxygen flowing to the brain and just move! The added bonus to this is that many employees will carry over their movements and incorporate them in to their daily routine to multiply the benefits! Of course, depending on your company's dress code, you may need to give your team the heads-up to make sure they're wearing proper attire.

25. Handwritten Note Hike

An old reliable play that never gets stale. A written "thank you" or "thinking of you" note received through the United States Postal Service is a cherished gem these days. It only takes a minute and a stamp, but this play goes long in endearing you to the recipient. Even a handwritten note left at the desk of your teammate wins bonus points because it is so rare. Think about it!

Pop Quiz! Which mail gets opened first?

1. A) A statement from a company that bills you monthly
2. B) A pre-printed solicitation letter with an offer
3. C) A handwritten note card with a real stamp

Ding! Ding! Ding! You win! Yes, the answer is C—the handwritten note card with a real stamp. Since email has taken over the world, this move is such a surprise it's almost a trick play. It will be treasured and displayed as a trophy.

Pro Tip: Buy blank note cards and stamps in advance so that there are no defensive tackles blocking your path for this Cheer Leadership tip. You can even order stamps online for delivery right to your doorstep. (Choosing stamps with a thoughtful theme or image often stands out as well.) When Jamie does something "noteworthy," don't hesitate, be deliberate and get that note in the mail right away. Get these tools and more in your Cheer Leadership kit at janspence.com.

26. Birthday Cake Block

It is a common practice in many workplaces to order birthday cake from the local grocery store bakery. However, you can boost this moment of acknowledgement even more! Give a gift that is personal to the staffer, budget allowing. Get to know the preferences of your employee. This makes them feel valued and that you see them as not only a worker, but also as a person. Maybe a book on gardening that they love or on being a new parent or perhaps a gift card to their favorite niche shop is the right play. Do the recon and it will be remembered for months after the sweet taste of cake is gone.

Pro Tip: To save time, have your reliable assistant or fellow staff person do the recon. Give them a budget, your credit card, and have them find the perfect item. You get the credit!

Block: when one player assertively places themselves in front of another player's path.

27. The Lunch Reverse

When was the last time you took your squad to lunch? Sometimes getting away from the work environment and having one-on-one time to bond is the only way to connect during the hectic day-to-day grind of the game. This is a great practice for co-workers as well.

We typically gravitate to those folks we are most comfortable with in the company. On most football teams, the offense hangs out together and the defense hangs out together. Nudge yourself and be intentional about practicing Cheer Leadership by having coffee or lunch with those you don't know well, possibly from other departments. Getting to know them on a personal level will only enhance everyone's level of play over time.

The reverse: a risky play in football in which multiple ball carriers take turns reversing the lateral direction of the football with each handoff.

28. The Press Box

One often overlooked tip is sharing compliments and praises from others (customers, prospects, co-workers, vendors, etc.) with the person who was actually praised! So often a customer will be leaving a store and say something like this to the nearest staff person: "Jenny was so friendly and helpful today. She was so patient with me as I made my decisions. She is a true gem for your company and the reason I shop here!" The staffer thanks the customer, and that's where the story usually ends. The buzzer sounds and game over.

Whenever you hear—or find out about—something like this, make sure Jenny knows! Be intentional about going to her and relating the kind words that were shared about her service and performance. If the affirming feedback from a customer or company executive was sent to you via email, promptly forward it to her. That reinforcement is powerful and will keep Jenny striving to perform at her highest level and exceeding expectations.

> **Pro Tip:** Not only will Jenny appreciate you sharing the compliment, she'll be a bigger fan when she sees you make a point to tell her boss and others about the kudos. Review other Cheer Leadership tips to find additional ways to commend Jenny when this occasion occurs and share your stories with us at info@janspence.com.

29. The Audible

In the hustle and bustle of busy days and ever-increasing work demands, we often neglect to stop and tell our peers how much we appreciate them. This one is a fan favorite! It just doesn't get any better than taking the time to look someone in the eye, call them by their name and genuinely say, "Thank you, Jade!" "I believe in you, Mary!" "Mikhael, I'm so proud of you!" or "Really great job with the way you handled that situation, Lisa!" Use this play often to let your teammates know that they matter.

Audible: when a football team's offense changes the play it is going to run at the last minute on the line of scrimmage. The quarterback literally shouts out code words to let his teammates know what he wants them to do.

FUN FACT! The Women's Football Alliance (WFA) is the largest women's tackle football league in the world. [24]

30. Friendly Fumble

Imagine how surprised your staff will be when you call an impromptu meeting, but instead of hearing the usual speech about how "we need to push harder to hit our goals," they find that it's friendly competition time! If you don't have a ping pong table or foosball game in your building, a board room or break room table will do for this tip.

A few decks of cards and a speed round of War will get the creative juices flowing as well as help everyone step away from the daily grind. Yahtzee is fun as well as Crazy Eights, dominoes or Go Fish which are also quick and easy options that anyone can play. See the Resources section for links to games and rules. R1 Get these tools and more in your Cheer Leadership kit at janspence.com.

Fumble: when a player who has possession and control of the ball loses it before they are tackled, go out of bounds or score.

Rookie Advice: Try to choose a time of day and day of the week when your staff most likely will not be in the middle of servicing customers or working on a tight deadline. Friday late afternoon or first thing Monday morning might be the perfect time for this "timeout." We all enjoy watching cheerleaders not only for their dazzling costumes and amazing stunts, but also because it takes us away from the intensity of the game. This fan-friendly break will accomplish the same.

Pro Tip: To save time, stock up at the local dollar store on playing cards, puzzles, games, and toys. Keep a basket or drawer full of your tricks to pull out at a moment's notice. Soon you'll be known for not only leading the team, but being the "fun boss" who keeps things light. After all, if we spend on average 90,000 hours in our lifetime at work, and it's not fun, why are we doing it?[25] We're happy to share winners on our social media feed, so be sure to send photos and winning stats to info@janspence.com.

31. Message on the Mirror Motion

Headed for a bio break? Grab that dry erase marker and your favorite quote. Write the quote or message of encouragement on the restroom mirror to inspire your team in an unexpected way. They'll appreciate the dose of inspiration while washing their hands and wondering who the mystery motivator is.

> **Pro Tip:** Here are several great resources to find quotes for just the right occasion.
>
> brainyquote.com
> quoteinvestigator.com
> thinkexist.com
> quodb.com

Get these tools and more in your Cheer Leadership kit at janspence.com.

> **Motion:** when an offensive player relocates by moving parallel to the line of scrimmage prior to the snap of the ball—designed to cause a one-on-one mismatch or mislead the defensive players.

32. Collaboration Catch

As simple as this may seem, people feel valued when you ask their opinion. Be intentional about inviting Candice, that new staff member or one who typically isn't part of the decision-making team, to sit in on the next planning meeting and offer a different perspective. Or make it a spur-of-the-moment invitation to your office to ask, "From your experience working with banks in the past, how would we best market to this new prospect?" They'll be floored and feel like they were the first draft pick because you remembered their background, expertise, and interests.

Often these new recruits have great ideas because they are fresh and they haven't been cooped up in the conference room repeatedly hearing the same suggestions bandied about! You may even tap in to their potential and identify a candidate for upward mobility—a possible new champion for Cheer Leadership!

Draft pick: one of the young prospects selected when each team takes turns picking players during the annual "draft" process.

---

33. Ice Cream Blitz

Who is not a fan of ice cream? A cooler full of everyone's favorite frosty treats will help melt away even the toughest day. Reward your crew with this surprise break. You can even invite your favorite customers over on a Friday afternoon for a big win. Recruit members of the team that may not get out of the office regularly and reward them with this hall pass to go purchase this concession stand staple. I haven't done the research, but I'm pretty sure no one has ever been able to eat ice cream and be upset about it!

> **Blitz:** the play where one or more extra defensive players join the linemen in rushing the quarterback, hoping to sack him—or her!—so that the offense loses yardage.

FUN FACT! In their inaugural season, the Jacksonville Dixie Blues went to the first Women's World Bowl I at Balboa Stadium in San Diego, California on February 24, 2002. They lost with a score of 34 – 20 to the California Quake.

34. The Team Uniform

Everyone loves new clothes. What if you adorned your team with a fresh cotton company T-shirt, especially if it means they can dress more casually at work? What is the message you want everyone to remember during a season of tight deadlines, long hours, tough work challenges, the dreaded annual audit, or grueling inventory? Put it on a T-shirt!

According to a study by Stormline, 61 percent of employees are more productive when the dress code is relaxed. [27]

Reinforce your current "cheer" (that project mantra such as "Attitude is everything!" "Think. Rethink. Action!" or football's "Clear eyes, full hearts, can't lose!") while increasing productivity as the clock ticks toward the end of the game.[28] Everyone loves fan gear and being dressed comfortably at work, and your staff will too.

> **Rookie Advice:** Since there are many body shapes, sizes, and style preferences, make sure you have a wide variety of shirt sizes (and possibly even styles or "fits") for a cross section of your team. Anyone can shrink a shirt with some hot water and a clothes dryer, but no one is going to take it to a tailor to have it expanded if it doesn't fit! Avoid losing fan points by trying to squeeze that XXXL-sized offensive lineman into that regular adult T!

Pro Tip: During the pre-season, ask your vendor for samples of shirts (or hats, smocks, bandanas, etc.) and get input from the beefiest defensive lineman to the leanest receiver to make sure you are ordering a cross section of sizes. However, if you're short on time and you decide on this form of Cheer Leadership at the last minute, know that there are companies available that are able to turn orders around extremely quickly. See the Resources section for some options. R2

35. Be the 12th Man

Look for opportunities to cheer everyone on! Hold the door open for others; restock the drinks in the breakroom fridge; smile and say, "Good day, Tamatha!" to everyone you pass; load paper in the copier when it is running low and start a fresh pot of coffee even if that's not your cup of tea. The opportunities are endless when you begin to be intentional about lifting others up.

The 12th Man: the powerful influence of the psychological, emotional "noise" of the fans at the game since football teams have 11 players.

FUN FACT: There have been 373 sets of brothers who have played in the NFL. There have been 217 sets of fathers and sons to play in the league.[26]

36. Article Highlight Reel

Show you care by forwarding an email or article that addresses a subject that you know your work partner will enjoy.

First, you have to know what's important to those with whom you spend 40-plus hours a week working alongside. There are many ways to uncover this insider information. Whether it's actually going for coffee together during a morning break, doing lunch or just asking casually after a meeting, "Hey, Devetrice, I never asked you about how you like to spend your weekends? What hobbies do you enjoy?" This information is valuable. Once you've played scout and have that insider knowledge, put your radar up and be on the lookout for cutting-edge related topics to share with your colleague.

> **Rookie Advice:** Stay positive and share articles that are uplifting and encouraging. Giving someone an article that could be seen as insulting, parochial or instructive like "Three Steps to Elevating Your Attire at Work" will not win friends nor influence your relationships with people in a helpful way!

37. Jumping Jacks

When you're preparing to tackle a big project or are in the heat of the battle, it's time for jumping jacks, combined with a battle cry! My football coach taught us in our pre-game warmup routine to follow a certain pattern of exercises led by our team captains. Near the end of the series of stretches, we would count our jumping jacks out loud in unison with the exception of the very last one. Instead of a typical numerical count-off at the end, we would flex our muscles, display our fiercest game face and growl like a pack of hound dogs! It inspired confidence within us and freaked out the other team with this unexpected "war cry!"

You can instill this same spirit within your group. Research backs this up. One study showed that athletes who scream when exerting themselves show an 11 percent increase in power output![29]

Having a motto, short phrase or "battle cry" that every one of your crew can shout out with conviction will deepen their commitment to the cause and the company while building courage to take on the sometimes seemingly impossible! In the front office, break room or out in the parking lot, gather the team for a good ol' pep rally with a battle cry! We want to cheer you on, so send us a video or your battle cry to info@janspence.com.

38. Personal Playbook

Most companies include a list of work anniversaries in the company newsletter, but how many truly make it a special occasion? The days of awarding the clock and ultimately the gold watch are long past. Even picking out "your special award" with your allotted number of points based on your pay grade and tenure just don't seem very personal any more.

What if you implemented an onboarding program where you photographed each new hire and even made recognition of their first 30 or 90 days with the company? Use some levity (Hey, this is all about Cheer Leadership and having fun, isn't it?) and shower that new hire with the "You found your way back to the office!" award for a month of consistent attendance. Or what about the "You survived boot camp" award for successfully making it through the 90-day initial period? Imagine the surprise and smile on your co-worker's face when they show up to the staff meeting and it's "Francesca Hudson" day as "Rookie of the Year." A photo of Francesca as the newbie on her first day is shared while the supervisor lauds how she has added value to the company and grown through her fresh start. Those personal compliments about how much Francesca is appreciated and how her contributions are valued will surely build loyalty so much more than the company newsletter mention among a list of others.

> **Rookie Advice:** A common practice is to pass around a greeting card for everyone to sign, but this is trite, takes little effort, and, let's be honest, the generic "personal" notes and pre-printed salutations may not mean much to the recipient. However, what if co-workers wrote a

word or phrase that describes what they appreciate most about Francesca on a photo frame mat? Consider including a photo with the entire team or a recent photo of Francesca placed in an inexpensive frame?

To get creative, there are online resources that can help you create a word cloud with the thoughts the team contributes to describe Francesca. See the Resources section for some options. R3 This will be one thing on the desk that is kept long after the company pen runs out of ink. It also stands as a tangible reminder to that employee that their coworkers value and appreciate them. This will help make sure the inspiration to live up to those expectations continues.

> **Pro Tip:** For the more executive positions, is an exclusive lunch with the company founder or a really nice, meaningful corporate gift in order? Perhaps they should receive a company credit card with their name on it. If Scott is known for always carrying cash, maybe a monogrammed money clip is ideal. If Raquel fancies a great cabernet, a custom-label wine bottle with accessories would surely bring a smile to her face.

39. No "Flags on This Play" Flowers

Imagine the surprise and buzz you'll create first thing in the morning when everyone shows up to a beautiful fresh daisy, carnation or rose on their desk? Your endorphins will kick in with the rush of knowing you delivered the anonymous flower power. You don't need to provide vases. Your crew will find a way to display this unexpected treasure—even an empty water bottle will work!

> **Pro Tip:** Warehouse stores like Sam's Club or Costco carry bulk flowers. If you have a local Flowerama store, you can purchase flowers by the stem at a great price. Otherwise, your local florist or grocery, drug or convenience store will work.

"Flag on the Play": when a referee tosses a yellow weighted cloth onto the field to signal that one of the rules of the game has been broken and that a team will receive a penalty.

FUN FACT! The Jacksonville Dixie Blues defeated the Indianapolis Vipers in 2002 to win their first Women's Football Alliance championship.

40. The Compliment Center

The power of words. You'll make someone's day when you notice them. Just a few simple words of "I really like that new print you hung in your office, Rafael," "I've noticed you're a really good communicator, Kathy," or "I appreciate how professional you are with our vendors, Tucker" always make people feel special just because you noticed and took the time to acknowledge them.

> **Rookie Advice:** Everyone must be careful in the work environment so that these compliments are not misconstrued. Be sure that your comments are pleasant and stick to simple, observable facts and are not suggestive or provocative. Don't be that obnoxious fan!

Center: the offensive lineman usually located in the middle who "hikes" the ball to the quarterback to begin each play.

41. The MVP (Most Valuable Player)

Set aside one week each quarter, twice a year, or even once annually during a special event (the company conference, picnic or holiday party) and place "MVP comment boxes" around the venue. Instruct your people to fill out "MVP sheets" naming their team players and sharing the reasons for a job well done. These sheets can be randomly selected and read aloud as part of the program, announcing to all what a great job people are doing within the organization. This Cheer Leadership tip isn't intended to identify a winner, but to acknowledge all who are leaving it on the field. Depending on the size of your team and its interpersonal dynamics, it might be wise to limit how many MVP sheets are read "publicly" about the same employee. See the Resources section for an example of a nomination sheet. R4

Pro Tip: To save time, you can buy lockable boxes from online retailers or your local office supply store instead of making your own. You want these to be secure so that someone who had too many adult beverages at the company party doesn't decide to investigate the kudos on their own!

42. Music Halftime Show

There are few joys in the world that can bring people together like music. While preferences will vary and it might be hard to get a team to agree, music helps us to feel alive. Keep the playing field fair by allowing each team player to choose the genre to be played on the office music system for a designated amount of time.

Or you can turn it up loud and take a music dance break where you forward the company phone lines, get out of your cubicle, close the break room door and just let everyone rock out in their own way.

> **Rookie Advice:** Be sensitive to lyrics to ensure that they are not offensive or disparaging to any people group. You'll have the human resources department flooding the field when they hear about that one! Play smart.

43. Social Media Screen Pass

Highlight individual accomplishments on company-approved social media sites. So often, companies share information that is primarily centered around the happenings of the organization and its products and services. Get personal! Assuming this is allowed through company policy, tag the employee's personal accounts so they are able to share their accolades with friends and family. The ripple effect of others close to them being able to further cheer them on will be a major hit. Some companies have internal network channels that function similarly to popular social media sites. Praises lauded through these means also win points.

Rookie Advice: Make sure that you are staying within corporate guidelines and always check with your communications department before posting. It's best to check with the recipient as well before tagging their personal accounts.

Screen Pass: a play in football in which a short pass is made to a running back or receiver who has positioned herself behind a small group (i.e. screen) of blockers.

44. The Opportunistic Offense

Remember that time you were new in a role and someone gave you that "insider tip" that made your job *so* much easier? Go on the offense and do the same for a colleague! When you see someone struggling, share that shortcut guide or little-known job hack. Just jump in and help them out!

Inviting Cedric out for a coffee break and explaining "the rules of the game" so that he ramps up more smoothly and fits into the company's culture will long be remembered by this rookie. You'll be lauded as his personal MVP when he realizes you have his best interests in mind.

> **Rookie Advice:** Make sure that your insider information is helpful and reflects positively on the company. Ensure it isn't viewed as gossip or "smashmouth" talk about fellow company members. Your newcomer will appreciate the heads up, but will likely view gossip as bad form and definitely against the rules of playing a clean game.

45. Substantive Sideline Chat

Make note of personal matters of your co-workers. The more you know about what is going on with them as a human being, the more you will be able to cheer them on!

Be intentional about asking, calling, or texting to ask about other things that aren't just work related. Questions like, "How'd your uncle's surgery go, Tyrone?" or "How's the little league team doing, Bianca?" go a long way in showing people that you care about them on a personal level.

FUN FACT! Football officially surpassed baseball as "America's Pastime" in 1965, when more people named it their favorite sport in the long-running Harris Poll on the subject. [30]

46. Ready. Set. Referee.

If the company picnic only comes once a year (and sadly, that is a fading tradition), it's hard to keep the buzz of bonding from the company softball game going for 364 days. Be confident in calling a flag on that play when the going gets tough. Blow the whistle and rally the troops to get outside the office.

Make an impromptu outing to the nearby sports grill to watch the national playoffs, catch the opening pitch at the local ball field, or just find the closest pool hall. And, no, not everyone will participate, but the pressure is on to show up for the draft next time, once everyone is talking about the laughs, the funny comments made, and what they learned about their teammates. Missing out on this insider information on their compadres will ensure that they won't want to miss the next field trip.

> **Rookie Advice:** If actually getting out of the office isn't logistically suitable, bring the game to the office! Have everyone wear their favorite team shirt and play an inside version of the sport. Fingertip football, for example, or hallway kickball are fun alternatives. See the Resources section for how to fold a fingertip football out of paper. R5

> **Pro Tip:** Save time and money by purchasing last minute tickets—you can often get a great deal. Or if you know the local farm team is a favorite, plan in advance by purchasing group tickets for the season. You'll be supporting your community and be assured you have

seats when the occasion arises. You can also use the "box seats" as an award for your employee of the week or as a random act of Cheer Leadership. These are perks that everyone loves, especially the xennials and millennials who value their social time as much as their work time.

Generation	Birth Years*
Silent	1937 – 1945
Baby Boomers	1946 – 1964
Generation X	1965 – 1980
Xennials**	1979 – 1985
Millennials/Generation Y	1981 – 1997
Generation Z	1998 – 2009
Generation Alpha	2010 – present

* Birth years may vary slightly depending upon the source.

**Xennials are a micro-generation that have characteristics of both Generation X and Generation Y. They remember the days before the internet, but have also easily adapted to and feel comfortable with the onset of new technology.

47. Rallying Red Zone

Okay, let's face it. Throughout the year, your group will appreciate your efforts to encourage them and, therefore, engagement and loyalty will increase. To mix things up, you may want to consider bringing in a "guest coach" to fire up the troops. It is critical that people know that you have their best interest and their career growth at heart, just as any faithful leader would. In addition, when you surprise them by bringing in a motivational speaker or local celebrity to pump them up before the big game, you'll elevate their level of energy and focus.

> **Pro Tip:** Yes, this is a shameless plug for the many professional speakers who have dedicated their careers and lives to inspiring others and lifting them up through their words. Your investment will be returned many times over as your team elevates their performance as a result of hearing from that "guest coach" and embracing their words of wisdom. Find just the right message for your team by locating a qualified motivator through the National Speakers Association at NSASpeaker.org. Links to the Global Speakers Federation can be found there as well.

Red Zone: the area between the goal line and the closest 20-yard line, which is the danger zone for the defense because the offense is so close to scoring.

48. Coffee Crowd Control

What better way is there to start a Monday morning after the weekend than with coffee that's superior to the standard office fare? If you make the effort to learn your team's favorite game time beverages, you'll score big points with this morning necessity. Whether it's Gatorade, energy drink, flavored hot tea or Starbucks, when the staff shows up to find their favorite mocha latte double pump with extra whip, productivity will soar!

FUN FACT! In 2006, the Jacksonville Dixie Blues had their first undefeated season after securing the national championship against the Tennessee Heat.

49. Listening Long Snap

One of the most overlooked, simple ways to encourage people, especially when they are struggling, is also one of the most powerful. *Listen*. Put down the phone, turn away from the keyboard, look someone in the eyes and truly listen! Being fully present and giving someone your undivided attention is a rare and cherished gift.

The best listeners seek to understand both what's being said verbally and what's being felt by the speaker. In his book *The Lost Art of Listening*, Michael P. Nichols explains that "the essence of good listening is empathy." You practice this by "entering into the experience of the other person." Use reflective listening skills to let your teammates know they are being heard and understood. Reflective listening is hearing what another person has said and then rephrasing back what you heard to make sure that you understood. The other person feels validated and knows that you comprehend what they were communicating.[31]

For example:
Juan: "I've got such tight deadlines, and we've got to get this proposal right to win the deal."
Linda: "It sounds like you're under a lot of pressure right now." (Reflects the emotions and rephrases what she just heard from Juan.)
Juan: "Exactly! A lot is hanging in the balance. Thanks for understanding."

In some cases, you may have to find the right time in the right place to ask how someone is doing, how things are going or how they are handling a challenging situation. Even though you may not be in a position to take action or improve someone's situation, just listening is a great Cheer Leadership tip during a tough time. Your gift of time and attention will earn a Super Bowl playoff position in their mind. People want to feel valued, heard, and appreciated and believe that they are making a difference.

> **Long Snap:** when the center hikes the football a longer distance for the punter, usually 15 yards, or the placeholder for field goal and extra point attempts, usually 7 yards.

Pro Tip: In many cases, there is a natural tendency to want to fix the situation, offer unsolicited advice or even minimize or dismiss the person's feelings, perspective, or concern. The Pro knows how to just listen without judgment, validate the other person, and reflect back what is being said without infusing their own opinion. Acknowledge the struggle with "That must be hard, Nika," "That is tough, Mateo," or "I'm sure you must be frustrated, Kara."

Avoid comparing their issue to your own experience or knowledge—don't share your own story of pain and how you conquered the challenge. Resist the temptation to be a "Monday morning quarterback" (a person who passes judgment and criticizes something after an event has occurred—i.e. telling the quarterback on

Monday morning how they should have played the game on Sunday). In this moment, be intentional about just listening so that you display the power of encouragement.

50. No Excessive Celebration Penalty on National Whatever Day

The real spirit of Cheer Leadership is encouraging others, boosting morale and having fun as a team! Did you know that every day has been deemed a national recognition day? Yes, there are actual holidays such as "Jamaican Patties Day," "Sneak Some Zucchini into Your Neighbor's Porch Day," "Wiggle Your Toes Day" and even "Chop Suey Day!"

You'll find one long list of the recognized reasons to be festive at NationalDayCalendar.com. To excel at this tip, find a really fun "National Day" that everyone would enjoy, mark the calendar, notify your troop and have fun! Be sure to take photos and email me at info@janspence.com so that I can share you in action with your squad!

Excessive Celebration: when a player exhibits conduct deemed unsportsmanlike when celebrating after a big play, resulting in a penalty. In 2017, the National Football League relaxed its rules so that players may celebrate with their teammates in creative ways that model fun and set good examples for the crowd.

51. Video Replay

Ever since the first YouTube clip was uploaded in 2005, fans have consistently gravitated to this user-friendly video-sharing site. Rather than sending the standard weekly email or printed memo update to your team, why not post a video with your most relevant news to refresh the communication experience? This will allow your squad to observe your always-important body language and tone. (Refer back to Tip No. 6 for more information on the communication formula.)

Today, viewers are used to seeing clips that are recorded on smartphones and posted directly online. Even national television shows often acquire these personal videos to share the latest breaking stories. So there's no need to call a timeout to stage a backdrop, wear a special outfit or even have a formal script. Just turn on your phone's video camera and speak! Choose your pep talk and speak from the heart. This will surely inspire the team, and they'll appreciate the break from the norm.

Currently, there are numerous options for video-sharing websites, including YouTube, Vimeo, Twitch, Metacafe, Flickr, Veoh, The Internet Archive, Crackle, Screen Junkies, Dailymotion and The Open Video Project.

> **Rookie Advice:** Be conscious that this internal video message could possibly be shared outside of the company, just as a newsletter or memo could. Ensure that you have corporate approval and are operating within company guidelines for this tip. One option for

privacy is to tag the videos as "unlisted" or "only the people with the private link can view" so the URL (address link) serves as the literal key. Since that link could be forwarded externally, be certain that the information contained is public-friendly.

Pro Tip: Short and sweet is best. If there is a lot of information to share, five minutes should be the maximum length for the recording. If it's a quick update or a request for action, keep the video under two minutes. It may take some practice, but you'll soon learn that you can say what you need to in a more concise manner. People appreciate brevity and directness. You'll also increase your view rate when they know that you respect their time and keep your videos succinct and on point.

52. Short Talk Strong Side

The stadium is packed with fans of the short talk format! A short talk is a speech given on one particular topic where the person shares their unique point of view. The maximum time frame for short talks is 18 minutes or less. Typically, the presenter focuses the communication of their idea to fit a targeted time frame of 18, 15, 8 or 5 minutes. The focus is very narrow which challenges the listener to think differently about the subject and hopefully take action. As an example, you can view my TEDx talk "What Football Taught Me about the Power of Words" at JanSpence.com.

Your team members have a wealth of knowledge, ideas and innovative ways to look at existing processes and challenges. Be sure to rotate team members so everyone gets a chance. You could choose a 5, 10, 15 or 18 minute format for your squad to share their ideas. Surely winning plays will come just from giving players an opportunity to think outside the box and come up with creative solutions that will improve the work environment.

> **Pro Tip:** Here's the best way to frame the short talk expectation to your participants. Lead by example and deliver the first talk. This will set the tone and elevate you as the coach who will run the plays. See the Resources section for specific guidelines on how to present a short talk. R6

Strong side: the side of the offensive line that has the most players to the left or right of the center. Often, this is the side with the tight end. Remember to visit janspence.com to get your Cheer Leadership Kit!

Conclusion

Ultimately, people want to feel valued, praised, acknowledged and encouraged as part of a team. By being intentional about connecting with your colleagues on a deeper level and encouraging them to do the same, you'll build relationships that last and create a stronger team and organization. As you consistently practice the tips in this playbook, "lifting up" others will soon become second nature. (Generally, it only takes about a month to establish a habit.) It's my hope that you will carry Cheer Leadership into other areas of your life and seek opportunities to encourage everyone around you, every day. Together, we can transform the world! I look forward to hearing about your "wins" soon!

30-Day Action Plan

To begin a new habit, one needs repetition and reinforcement. This 30-day action plan will help you use the tips you choose to start exercising that encouragement muscle. By implementing tips frequently in the first thirty days, you'll become more aware of opportunities and be on your way to being an MVP of Cheer Leadership! You don't have to utilize a "bigger" tip such as taking the team to a ball game or having a potluck lunch every day, but you can implement compliments, praise, asking personalized questions, and smiling on a daily basis! And, it's easy to do!

Choose a simple tip now and write it in the box below.

Set a start date to practice Cheer Leadership and put that in the corresponding box.

On the morning of the date you choose, put five or six paper clips (coins or some other simple small portable items can also be used) in your left pocket. Throughout the day those items in your pocket will be your reminder to practice using your Cheer Leadership tip.

For tips that can be used multiple times in one day, move one paper clip from your left pocket to your right pocket each time you execute the encouraging tip. This serves as a reminder to be intentional about cheering on your team and also reinforces the progress you've made through the day. If you have clips leftover at the end of the day, just start anew the next morning! This can also be spread throughout the week for tips that take a little more time each day.

Tip Used	Date Used	Notes

Tip Used	Date Used	Notes

Tip Used	Date Used	Notes

Encouragement Scoreboard

This section is designed to encourage you to use a variety of Cheer Leadership tips throughout the year. By writing down what you actually did, when you did it, what the outcome was, and ideas for the future, you will reinforce the benefit of encouraging your people and sharpen your own skills over time. Remember to send ideas, photos and comments to info@janspence.com!

Tip Used	Date	Impact/Outcome	Ideas for the Future

Tip Used	Date	Impact/Outcome	Ideas for the Future

Tip Used	Date	Impact/Outcome	Ideas for the Future

Tip Used	Date	Impact/Outcome	Ideas for the Future

Tip Used	Date	Impact/Outcome	Ideas for the Future

Tip Used	Date	Impact/Outcome	Ideas for the Future

Tip Used	Date	Impact/Outcome	Ideas for the Future

Tip Used	Date	Impact/Outcome	Ideas for the Future

Tip Used	Date	Impact/Outcome	Ideas for the Future

Tip Used	Date	Impact/Outcome	Ideas for the Future

Tip Used	Date	Impact/Outcome	Ideas for the Future

Tip Used	Date	Impact/Outcome	Ideas for the Future

Tip Used	Date	Impact/Outcome	Ideas for the Future

Tip Used	Date	Impact/Outcome	Ideas for the Future

Tip Used	Date	Impact/Outcome	Ideas for the Future

Tip Used	Date	Impact/Outcome	Ideas for the Future

Tip Used	Date	Impact/Outcome	Ideas for the Future

Resources

R1: The United States Playing Card Company, creator of the iconic BICYCLE® brand, has been creating the world's best playing cards for over 130 years. Their website has a plethora of rules for card games, including classics like Solitaire, Bridge, Spades, and all forms of Poker, to some of the lesser known games like Red Dog, Peep Nap, and Presidents. For more details, visit: bicyclecards.com/rules

R2: Unify your team and create a cohesive vibe by ordering custom shirts, hats, drawstring bags, or other apparel. Use your company logo or tagline or mix it up and use one of the favorite "quotes of the day" from Tip #5!

custommink.com
brokenarrowwear.com
undergroundshirts.com

Need something with a quick turnaround time? Check out rushordertees.com.

R3: Creating word clouds has never been easier! The following programs allow you to quickly and easily input your specific words, add your own personal flair, and create a piece of office art that is sure to inspire Cheer Leadership! Best of all, they are all free to use!

wordclouds.com
wordle.net
worditout.com/word-cloud/create

R4: Please feel free to download this form at janspence.com.

MVP NOMINATION FORM

I'd like to nominate:

(Check one):

___ as player of the game (made some stellar plays this year)

___ for leaving it all on the field all the time (consistent & reliable)

___ as rookie of the year (excelled at something new under pressure)

Why they are worthy:

Nominated by:

(Note: Unsigned forms will not be considered.)

R5: Thanks to the power of the World Wide Web, you can create a mini football out of a regular sheet of 8.5×11" paper in less than a minute and spark some friendly competition by starting your own game of "fingertip football" in the office! For detailed instructions with pictures, visit wikihow.com/Make-a-Paper-Football

R6: Even a short five-minute presentation can lose the audience's attention if it isn't prepared and presented properly. To help keep you on track, here are some guidelines to keep in mind. Most importantly, remember to honor your allotted time!

business.tutsplus.com/tutorials/5-minute-presentation–cms-29182

pophealth.wisc.edu/sites/default/files/
quick_tips_to_a_successful_10_minute_talk_and_effective_ppt_
presentation.pdf
ww2.amstat.org/meetings/jsm/2014/
effectivepresentations.cfm

Appendix

1. "Innovation lessons from Pixar: An interview with Oscar-winning ...." Accessed August 28, 2018. mckinsey.com/business-functions/strategy-and-corporate-finance/our-insights/innovation-lessons-from-pixar-an-interview-with-oscar-winning-director-brad-bird.
2. "Workplace Stress – American Institute of ...." Accessed August 28, 2018. stress.org/workplace-stress/.
3. "Empowering middle managers is central to ... – The Jostle Blog." Accessed August 28, 2018. blog.jostle.me/blog/empowering-middle-managers-is-central-to-employee-engagement.
4. "Obesity and overweight – World Health Organization." Accessed August 28, 2018. who.int/news-room/fact-sheets/detail/obesity-and-overweight.
5. "Employee Appreciation Survey – Glassdoor." Accessed August 28, 2018. glassdoor.com/press/employees-stay-longer-company-bosses-showed-appreciation-glassdoor-survey/.
6. "Immaculate Reception – Wikipedia." Accessed August 28, 2018. en.wikipedia.org/wiki/Immaculate_Reception.
7. "Benefits of Plants in The Office – NORTEC." Accessed August 28, 2018. nortec.org.au/benefits-of-plants-in-the-office/.
8. "The 15 Best Plants for Your Office and the Science ... – ProFlowers." Accessed August 28, 2018. proflowers.com/blog/office-plants.
9. "Fun Facts About Cheerleading History – ThoughtCo." Accessed August 28, 2018. thoughtco.com/cheerleading-history-4080643.
10. "List of National Football League head coaches with 50 wins – Wikipedia." Accessed August 28, 2018.

en.wikipedia.org/wiki/
List_of_National_Football_League_head_coaches_with_50_
wins.

11. "Amazon.com: Nonverbal Communication
(9780202309668): Albert ...." Accessed August 28, 2018.
amazon.com/Nonverbal-Communication-Albert-
Mehrabian/dp/0202309665.

12. "Brief diversions vastly improve focus, researchers find —
ScienceDaily." Accessed August 28, 2018. sciencedaily.com/
releases/2011/02/110208131529.htm.

13. "Fun Facts About Cheerleading History – ThoughtCo."
Accessed August 28, 2018. thoughtco.com/cheerleading-
history-4080643.

14. "12 Science-Backed Reasons You Should Make Friends at
Work ...." Accessed August 28, 2018. getvoip.com/blog/2018/
01/03/benefits-of-work-friends/.

15. "How to Win Friends & Influence People: Dale Carnegie ... –
Amazon.com." Accessed August 28, 2018. amazon.com/
How-Win-Friends-Influence-People/dp/0671027034.

16. "How does sugar affect my brain? | Well+Good." Accessed
August 28, 2018. wellandgood.com/good-food/how-sugar-
affects-the-brain-cognitive-function/.

17. "Fun Facts About Cheerleading History – ThoughtCo."
Accessed August 28, 2018. thoughtco.com/cheerleading-
history-4080643.

18. "3 Reasons Promoting From Within Is Better for Growing ...
– Entrepreneur." Accessed August 28, 2018.
entrepreneur.com/article/274346.

19. "Fun Facts About Cheerleading History – ThoughtCo."
Accessed August 28, 2018. thoughtco.com/cheerleading-
history-4080643.

20. "New Study Proves That Laughter Really Is The Best
Medicine | HuffPost." Accessed August 28, 2018.
huffingtonpost.com/2014/04/22/laughter-and-
memory_n_5192086.html.

21. "Fun Facts About Cheerleading History – ThoughtCo." Accessed August 28, 2018. thoughtco.com/cheerleading-history-4080643.

22. "Protein Foods – Dr. Axe." Accessed August 28, 2018. draxe.com/protein-foods/.

23. "Effect of frequent interruptions of prolonged sitting on self-perceived ...." Accessed August 28, 2018. ijbnpa.biomedcentral.com/articles/10.1186/s12966-016-0437-z.

24. "Mission – WOMEN'S FOOTBALL ALLIANCE." Accessed August 28, 2018. wfaprofootball.com/about/.

25. "1/3 of your life is spent at work – Gettysburg College." Accessed August 28, 2018. gettysburg.edu/news_events/press_release_detail.dot?id=79db7b34-630c-4f49-ad32-4ab9ea48e72b.

26. "101 amazing NFL facts that will blow your mind | For The Win." Accessed August 28, 2018. ftw.usatoday.com/2015/10/101-amazing-nfl-facts-that-will-blow-your-mind.

27. "61% of employees more productive when dress code is relaxed, study ...." Accessed August 28, 2018. recruitment-international.co.uk/blog/2017/01/61-percent-of-employees-more-productive-when-dress-code-is-relaxed-study-finds.

28. "Peter Berg reveals the inspiration behind "Clear Eyes, Full Hearts ...." Accessed August 28, 2018. sports.yahoo.com/news/peter-berg-reveals-the-inspiration-behind-clear-eyes-full-hearts-cant-lose-215844638.html.

29. "20 Battle Cries of Warriors Through the Ages | The Art of Manliness." Accessed August 28, 2018. artofmanliness.com/articles/battle-cries/.

30. "101 amazing NFL facts that will blow your mind | For The Win." Accessed August 28, 2018. ftw.usatoday.com/2015/10/101-amazing-nfl-facts-that-will-blow-your-mind.

31. "The Lost Art of Listening: Second Edition: How ... – Guilford Press." Accessed August 28, 2018. guilford.com/books/The-Lost-Art-of-Listening/Michael-Nichols/9781593859862.

About the Author

Jan Spence is an international speaker, trainer and consultant who has taught around the globe in countries such as Panama, Romania, Switzerland, Uganda and Australia. She and her husband of eighteen years, Mitch, launched the second FiltaFry franchise in the U.S. in 2003. As CEO, Jan built such a successful operation that they were awarded the "2005 Franchisee of the Year" by the International Franchise Association. Meeting their four-year plan, they sold the business in 2007 at 300 percent ROI.

A former professional football player, Jan learned how the power of encouraging others triggers positive action. In her TEDx talk, "What Football Taught Me About the Power of Words" (online at JanSpence.com), she combines those lessons with her business acumen to inspire people to make a difference through Cheer Leadership—a methodology that consistently inspires a positive transformation in businesses and individuals.

Jan's expertise—combined with her Southern charm, quick wit and an exuberant personality—has contributed to prolific success in diverse aspects of business, sales and life. As an award-winning speaker and professional member of the National Speakers Association, this good-humored optimist creates memorable, energizing presentations that are impactful and customized for every audience. With an entertaining style that is PowerPoint-free, Jan motivates and promotes change—for the best.

Jan serves on the boards of Meeting Professionals International—North Florida and Compass Finances God's Way—Florida. A faithful alumna of Mercer University and Alpha

Delta Pi Sorority, she is active with the Association of Talent Development and Beach Church in Jacksonville, Florida. She and her husband enjoy traveling the world when not at home cheering on their favorite teams, attending cultural events or playing cards.

Connect with us:
facebook.com/janspenceassociates
linkedin/com/in/jan-spence
twitter.com/janhspence
youtube.com/janspenceassociates

14001 Cashon Falls Ct.
Jacksonville, FL 32224
904-821-9309 (o); 904-821-2109 (f)
janspence.com
jan@janspence.com

Made in the USA
Columbia, SC
30 December 2018